DISCOVER
JESUS

12 Week Introductory Course

discover**jesus**.today

Discover Jesus Leader's Guide
A 12 Week Introduction Course by Geoff Woodcock

The Discover Jesus Leader's Guide and Workbook are both available on our website for downloading and printing. If you would like to view more resources, start a Discover Jesus group, or connect with our team, please visit our website or email us:

Web | www.discoverjesus.today
Email | info@discoverjesus.today

ISBN 978-0-9941333-1-1
Version 1 (February 2016)
Published by Acacia.Media
Printed in the USA. US English spellings used.

Contents

Introduction

The Discover Jesus course is a 12 week introduction course looking at who God is, who we are, and what it means to follow God. The course is designed for groups but can be done one-on-one or even individually. If you are working through the course material by yourself, get a copy of the Leader's Guide and refer to it as you do the questions in the workbook.

The course is based around passages from the Bible. For a brief overview of what the Bible is all about, head to the back section on page 131.

During the studies we make use of a lot of questions. The questions are designed to get you thinking about what the Bible is saying. If you are in a group, please be encouraged to participate and say what you think. Don't be afraid of getting an answer wrong—it's not a case right or wrong, but simply thinking things through together. If you find yourself answering all the questions, try to make space for other people in the group to have a say as well.

Each week there is some reading and some questions to do at home. They don't take long and you can check them off as you go. If you don't have a Bible, ask your group leader for one or find one online. We have links to some online Bibles at our website: www.discoverjesus.today.

Enjoy!

1 | Creator God

In the Beginning

Genesis 1:1, 26-27

[1] In the beginning, God created the heavens and the earth… [26] Then God said, "Let us make man in our image, after our likeness. And let them have dominion over the fish of the sea and over the birds of the heavens and over the livestock and over all the earth and over every creeping thing that creeps on the earth." [27] So God created man in his own image, in the image of God he created him; male and female he created them.

Q: What does it mean to be created? What is our purpose as humans in life?

Q: What does the world tell us about our purpose in life? What are we taught is the reason for our existence?

Q: Can we make up our own purpose for our life? Can we define our reason for being ourselves?

Psalm 139:13-14

¹³ For You formed my inward parts;

You wove me in my mother's womb.

¹⁴ I will give thanks to You, for I am fearfully [awesomely] and wonderfully made;

Wonderful are Your works,

And my soul knows it very well.

Q: What does this passage tell you about the value of your life?

" As people, we were not created by chance. Not a single feature of the awesome complexity that is human life came about as a result of random changes in nature. Every part of us: body, soul and spirit has been deliberately designed and wonderfully made by God. And if we are deliberately designed by God, it is because He has a definite purpose for us. He has a reason for giving us life.

With this in mind, the goal of this course is basically to explore these questions:

1. Who is God?
2. Who are we?
3. Who did God create us to be?

God of the Heavens

Psalm 113:4-6

⁴ The LORD is high above all nations;

His glory is above the heavens.

⁵ Who is like the LORD our God,

Who is enthroned on high,

⁶ Who humbles Himself to behold

The things that are in heaven and in the earth?

Q: What does it mean for God to humble Himself? Why is humility important for God?

" The universe is made up of countless stars and planets within countless galaxies. We can't get our minds around the billions of stars in our own galaxy, let alone imagine the incredible scale of the entire universe.

We are so small and insignificant that we exalt ourselves to study the stars. Yet God is so infinitely great that He has to humble Himself just to look upon the universe that exists so far beneath Him. Why? Because God is the Creator, the universe is created. God is spiritual, the universe is material. God is eternal, the universe is temporal. God is infinite, and the universe is finite. So God has to humble Himself to look at a physical universe that exists on a level inexpressibly far below His eternal glory.

Q: If we cannot even comprehend the creation, how can we possibly comprehend the Creator?

Q: If we cannot comprehend God then how can we possibly come to know God?

Summary

" God created us with a clearly defined purpose. However, we cannot discover God or His purposes for us by ourselves. He is too awesome for our minds to conceive. The only way we can discover who God is and why He has created us is if He makes Himself and His purposes known to us.

And that is exactly what He has done. God has been working throughout history to reveal Himself and the Bible has recorded some amazing insights into the nature and purposes of God. But His ultimate purpose for humanity was kept secret until a specific time: the time of Love. At that time God would reveal Himself in a new and amazing way. He would express His love and display His nature as it had never been seen before. He would reveal what He is really like and it would change the world forever.

1| Home Reading and Questions

☐ **Isaiah 40:21-31**
Take some time one evening to look at the stars above. There are only around 2000 stars visible on a clear night with the naked eye. Using current technology, astronomers roughly estimate there are more than 70 billion trillion (7x10²²) stars in the universe, and countless planets.

I: Imagine a God who could create all the stars and give each and every star a name. Imagine a God who needs to humble Himself just to look at His stars. Imagine that this great God intentionally created you.

Q: How is it even possible that God would know every star *by name*?

Q: Why would God create me?

☐ **Matthew 6:25-34, Matthew 10:26-33**
Take some time to imagine a God who knows us so well that He has numbered every hair on our heads. God is a God of details. He takes time to name the stars and to count the hairs. He cares for us more than we can know or understand.

I: Imagine a God who deeply loves you and cares for you. Imagine the Creator of the Universe personally promising to look after you and give you everything you need in life.

Q: What do I really need?

Q: What would it be like to never have to worry about anything ever again?

☐ **Psalm 139**

God fills the entire earth and universe with His presence. There is nowhere we can go to escape His presence. God has always been present with us at every point in our lives, regardless of whether we knew it or not.

I: Imagine a God that knows every word and every thought before you do. Imagine a God who knew you before He created you and who is intimately aware of everything you think, say and do. Imagine a God of love, powerful enough to bring His love into every detail of your life.

Q: Has God really been with me my entire life?

Q: Why does God so much care about me?

Q: How can I receive God's love?

☐ **Prayer** God, if this is all true and you are really with me, then please show me and help me to believe. If you are real then please reveal yourself to me. If you created me then please show me why.

☐ **John 1- John 3**
Write down your questions here:

☐ Experiences with God

Write down your some of your own prayers, discoveries, questions and experiences.

2 | Jesus

Jesus' Birth Foretold

In the Bible, a prophet is someone who God would speak clearly to. The job of the prophet was to relay God's word to people, cities and nations. In 730BC God spoke to a prophet called Isaiah and revealed that God would send a child, who would become a king over His people forever.

Over 700 years later that child was born to a young woman named Mary in a small town called Bethlehem. Mary named the child *Jesus*. In the Bible, the books of Matthew, Mark, Luke and John (also known as the gospels or good news) tell of Jesus' life and teachings.

Isaiah 7:14
Therefore the Lord himself will give you a sign. Behold, the virgin shall conceive and bear a son, and shall call his name Immanuel [meaning *God with us*].

Matthew 1:18-23
[18] Now the birth of Jesus Christ took place in this way. When his mother Mary had been betrothed to Joseph, before they came together she was found to be with child from the Holy Spirit. [19] And her husband Joseph, being a just man and unwilling to put her to shame, resolved to divorce her quietly. [20] But as he considered these things, behold, an angel of the Lord appeared to him in a dream, saying, "Joseph, son of David, do not fear to take Mary as your wife, for that which is conceived in her is from the Holy Spirit. [21] She will bear a son, and you shall call his name Jesus, for he will save his people from their sins." [22] All this took place to fulfill what the Lord had spoken by the prophet:

[23] "Behold, the virgin shall conceive and bear a son, and they shall call his name Immanuel" (which means, God with us).

Q: How could Isaiah know 700 years beforehand that Jesus would be born?

Q: Why did God send Jesus?

Luke 2:21-32 (NASB)

[21] And when eight days had passed, before His circumcision, His name was then called Jesus, the name given by the angel before He was conceived in the womb. [22] And when the days for their purification according to the law of Moses were completed, they brought Him up to Jerusalem to present Him to the Lord [23] (as it is written in the Law of the Lord, "every firstborn male that opens the womb shall be called holy to the Lord"), [24] and to offer a sacrifice according to what was said in the Law of the Lord, "a pair of turtledoves or two young pigeons."

[25] And there was a man in Jerusalem whose name was Simeon; and this man was righteous and devout, looking for the consolation of Israel; and the Holy Spirit was upon him. [26] And it had been revealed to him by the Holy Spirit that he would not see death before he had seen the Lord's Christ. [27] And he came in the Spirit into the temple; and when the parents brought in the child Jesus, to carry out for Him the custom of the Law, [28] then he took Him into his arms, and blessed God, and said, [29] "Now Lord, You are releasing Your bond-servant to depart in peace, According to Your word; [30] For my eyes have seen Your salvation, [31] which You have prepared in the presence of all peoples, [32] a light of revelation to the Gentiles, and the glory of Your people Israel."

Q: Why is Jesus called a light of revelation? What is He revealing?

Q: Who is Jesus revealing God to?

Jesus: The Light of Revelation

Matthew 11:25-27

[25]At that time Jesus declared, "I thank you, Father, Lord of heaven and earth, that you have hidden these things from the wise and understanding and revealed them to little children; [26]yes, Father, for such was your gracious will. [27]All things have been handed over to me by my Father, and no one knows the Son except the Father, and no one knows the Father except the Son and anyone to whom the Son chooses to reveal him.

Q: Who is the Father that Jesus is talking about?

Q: Why is Jesus the only one who knows the Father?

Q: What does it mean for Jesus to reveal God to us?

Q: How does Jesus reveal God to us?

Q: What does it mean to become like little children?

Q: Is there any way that we could get to know God apart from Jesus?

Revealing God

" Jesus reveals the Father through His teaching and His life. In this section we'll look at some of Jesus' teachings and how they show us what God is like.

Revealing a God of Love

Matthew 22:34-40

[34] But when the Pharisees heard that he had silenced the Sadducees, they gathered together. [35] And one of them, a lawyer, asked him a question to test him. [36] "Teacher, which is the great commandment in the Law?" [37] And he said to him, "You shall love the Lord your God with all your heart and with all your soul and with all your mind. [38] This is the great and first commandment. [39] And a second is like it: You shall love your neighbor as yourself. [40] On these two commandments depend all the Law and the Prophets."

Q: What does Jesus' teaching here show us about God?

" All the commandments of the Bible and all the prophecies depend entirely on love. That means when we read a command in Scripture, we need to interpret it through the lens of love. Without love, we have only legalism: a stressful life in which we strive in vain to keep the rules and commands of Scripture. However with love, we have the power of God's nature within us, which leads us to do good works *naturally and willingly*.

Revealing a God who Provides

Luke 12:22-31

[22] And he said to his disciples, "Therefore I tell you, do not be anxious about your life, what you will eat, nor about your body, what you will put on. [23] For life is more than food, and the body more than clothing. [24] Consider the ravens: they neither sow nor reap, they have neither storehouse nor barn, and yet God feeds them. Of how much more value are you than the birds! [25] And which of you by being anxious can add a single hour to his span of life? [26] If then you are not able to do as small a thing as that, why are you anxious about the rest? [27] Consider the lilies, how they grow: they neither toil nor spin, yet I tell you, even Solomon in all his glory was not arrayed like one of these. [28] But if God so clothes the grass, which is alive in the field today, and tomorrow is thrown into the oven, how much more will he clothe you, O you of little faith! [29] And do not seek what you are to eat and what you are to drink, nor be worried. [30] For all the nations of the world seek after these things, and your Father knows that you need them. [31] Instead, seek his kingdom, and these things will be added to you.

Q: What does this teaching show us about God?

Revealing a God who Heals

Matthew 8:1-3

[1] When Jesus came down from the mountain, large crowds followed Him. [2] And a leper came to Him and bowed down before Him, and said, "Lord, if You are willing, You can make me clean." [3] Jesus stretched out His hand and touched him, saying, "I am willing; be cleansed." And immediately his leprosy was cleansed.

Q: What does this passage reveal about God?

" It is interesting to note that at the time leprosy was considered to be highly contagious and so no one would touch or even go near a leper for fear of the disease. Lepers led lonely lives, isolated from people and void of physical connection. It was a physically, psychologically, socially and emotionally crushing condition. Jesus had previously healed many people just by speaking out the words. But in this case He reached out His hand and touched the untouchable. By doing so, Jesus revealed not only the power of God, but the tender love and compassion of God.

Revealing a God who Forgives (if time allows)

Luke 17:1-4

¹ And he said to his disciples, "Temptations to sin are sure to come, but woe to the one through whom they come! ² It would be better for him if a millstone were hung around his neck and he were cast into the sea than that he should cause one of these little ones to sin.

³ Pay attention to yourselves! If your brother sins, rebuke him, and if he repents, forgive him, ⁴ and if he sins against you seven times in the day, and turns to you seven times, saying, 'I repent,' you must forgive him."

Q: What does it mean to sin?

Q: What does this teaching tell us about God?

Summary

In the Old Testament, God primarily revealed Himself through prophets: people He would speak to clearly who would then relay His word to the people. But then, at the perfect time, God revealed Himself in the person of Jesus Christ. The things that Jesus did, the teachings Jesus shared, and the life He led, all reveal something of the awesome nature of God to us.

To really get this revelation, we need to become like little children in our hearts. We need to lay aside our skepticism, our agendas, our biases and hang-ups, and just listen to really hear what Jesus has to say. If we can take Jesus at His word then He will not only reveal the Father to us, but He will also show us exactly why God created us.

2 | Home Reading and Questions

□ **Matthew 9:10-13**

The Pharisees were religious leaders of the Jewish people. They were offended that Jesus would spend time with sinners—people who would regularly act against the loving nature of God. Some of these people like the tax collectors would cheat, lie and steal as a way of life. Some were prostitutes. Some were alcoholics. There were many who were hooked on the self-destructive pleasures of life. The Pharisees were worried that hanging out with such people would drag them down into sin. But Jesus saw the whole situation differently.

Q: What does this Bible passage teach me about the nature of God?

Q: Why would Jesus want to spend time with people if they were sinners?

Q: What does Jesus mean "I desire compassion, and not sacrifice"?

Q: Would Jesus want to hang out with me?

☐ **Luke 15:1-10**

The Pharisees still can't get over the fact that Jesus spends so much time with sinners. Here Jesus decides to tackle the issue head-on. He shows us that God does not write-off people who go their own way and do their own thing. Instead He seeks us out. He searches for us like a lost coin, and like a shepherd searching for a lost sheep, Jesus keeps on calling out to us until He finds us.

Q: Have I gone my own way in life?

Q: Is God really searching for me?

Q: Can I sense God calling me to come to Him?

I: Imagine being a young person whose fiancée has got lost on a hike. How hard would you search to find your true love? Or imagine being a father or mother, whose only child is lost. Would you ever give up the search for your lost child?

Now imagine God. A God who never tires, and who never gives up the search for the one He loves. Imagine a God of unfailing love, relentlessly calling out your name. Imagine yourself lost. Where are you? Are you running and trying to find your own way to safety? Have you stopped running? Or are you turning towards the sound of the voice?

☐ **Prayer** God, if you're really searching for me, can you help me to hear your call? Can you help me to know in my heart that you love me and that you'll take care of me?

☐ **John 4 - John 6**
Write down your questions here:

☐ **Experiences with God**

Write down your some of your own prayers, discoveries, questions and experiences.

3 | The Father of Love

"" In the last study we looked at some of the ways Jesus revealed the Father. In this study we are going to focus on one specific teaching in which Jesus not only reveals what God is like, but also reveals what we are like.

The Father's Heart

Luke 15:11-32

[11] And he said, "There was a man who had two sons. [12] And the younger of them said to his father, 'Father, give me the share of property that is coming to me.' And he divided his property between them. [13] Not many days later, the younger son gathered all he had and took a journey into a far country, and there he squandered his property in reckless living. [14] And when he had spent everything, a severe famine arose in that country, and he began to be in need. [15] So he went and hired himself out to one of the citizens of that country, who sent him into his fields to feed pigs. [16] And he was longing to be fed with the pods that the pigs ate, and no one gave him anything.

[17] "But when he came to himself, he said, 'How many of my father's hired servants have more than enough bread, but I perish here with hunger! [18] I will arise and go to my father, and I will say to him, "Father, I have sinned against heaven and before you. [19] I am no longer worthy to be called your son. Treat me as one of your hired servants."' [20] And he arose and came to his father. But while he was still a long way off, his father saw him and felt compassion, and ran and embraced him and kissed him. [21] And the son said to him, 'Father, I have sinned against heaven and before you. I am no longer worthy to be called your son.' [22] But the father said to his servants, 'Bring quickly the best robe, and put it on him, and put a ring on his hand, and shoes on his feet. [23] And bring the fattened calf and kill it, and let us eat and celebrate. [24] For this my son was dead, and is alive again; he was lost, and is found.' And they began to celebrate.

²⁵ "Now his older son was in the field, and as he came and drew near to the house, he heard music and dancing. ²⁶ And he called one of the servants and asked what these things meant. ²⁷ And he said to him, 'Your brother has come, and your father has killed the fattened calf, because he has received him back safe and sound.' ²⁸ But he was angry and refused to go in. His father came out and entreated him, ²⁹ but he answered his father, 'Look, these many years I have served you, and I never disobeyed your command, yet you never gave me a young goat, that I might celebrate with my friends. ³⁰ But when this son of yours came, who has devoured your property with prostitutes, you killed the fattened calf for him!' ³¹ And he said to him, 'Son, you are always with me, and all that is mine is yours. ³² It was fitting to celebrate and be glad, for this your brother was dead, and is alive; he was lost, and is found.'"

> This story is one of many parables in the Bible. A parable is a metaphor—a story loaded with symbolism that can deliver a deeper message straight to the heart. However, if we miss the symbolism then we miss the message. So we need to slow down and take some time with the story to think about what Jesus is really saying.

Q: Who is the father in the parable?

Q: Who are the sons?

Q: What does this parable reveal about God?

The Younger Son

Q: What was the younger son missing out on while he lived in the far country?

Q: Why did the younger son leave in the first place?

> When the younger son left his family behind, he also disconnected himself from his identity within the family. He went to a land where he would not be recognized, where he could be free to indulge in wasteful living. He denied who he was—his place in his family and community—all in the pursuit of pleasure.

Q: Why did he return?

Q: Do you think he would have returned if there was no famine?

Q: What was his plan?

Q: What does this tell us about his identity?

Q: What does this mean for us?

Q: What happened when the Father saw the son coming?

Q: What is Jesus telling us about God?

Q: Why does the Father love the son so much? Does the younger son deserve the Father's love?

Q: Did the younger son offer himself as a servant to his father as he had planned?

Q: Why not?

Q: What does the robe represent?

Q: What does the ring represent?

Q: What do the sandals represent?

Q: What did they do to celebrate?

Q: So what does all this tell us about God?

The Elder Son

" The story that Jesus told is about the father's love for both of his sons. The elder son is quite different from his brother. He didn't leave home. He didn't waste his life pursuing pleasure. He worked hard to please his father at home. But with the return of the younger son and the celebrations that began, an underlying anger rose up within the elder son.

Q: Why did the elder son get angry?

Q: What was the father's response?

Q: If everything that the father had was shared with the elder son then what was the problem? Why didn't the elder son take a young goat to enjoy with his friends?

" The elder son represents those people who have made their personal religion one of "doing the right things" (and "not doing the wrong things"). Deep down the elder son believed that the affection and approval of his father needed to be earned through obedience. So he called his father to look at how much he had done for him: "Look, these many years I have served you, and I never disobeyed your command, yet you never gave me a young goat, that I might celebrate with my friends". The son believed that he had done enough to earn his father's blessing, whereas the younger son had done nothing at all to earn it. So it didn't seem fair when the father lavished the younger son with love, affection and approval. That kind of love seemed offensive.

Q: Did the father love the elder son any less than the younger?

Q: So why did the elder son not enjoy the riches that were his?

Q: What does this show us about ourselves?

Q: Is it possible to go our own way in life, but still enjoy the Father's love and blessing?

Q: Is it possible to follow God and still miss out on the blessing of being His son?

Q: Who do you relate to within the story?

Summary

When Jesus shared this parable, He was revealing the heart of God to us. He wasn't condemning either son for the choices they had made, but used each son to highlight a different aspect of God's love for us. The younger son wasted his life and the inheritance that God had given him. When he realized what he had done he turned back to God and found God already waiting and watching for him, with arms of love wide open. The unconditional love of God swept over the son. His old life of selfishness was washed away in the Father's love and a new life of blessing, honor, and privilege began.

The elder son refused to celebrate. He had spent his life trying to earn God's blessing and approval, only to be told that he always had it. He simply had to ask for whatever he wanted and the Father would have gladly given it to him.

What Jesus is revealing to us about God is that the Father loves us with an unfailing, unchanging, unshakeable love. He won't give up on us. He will keep calling us and waiting for us until we come to Him, and then He will shower us with His love. He will accept us back into His family completely and unconditionally. As children of God, we can then enjoy all the awesome family benefits given to us by our Heavenly Father. We can live in the blessing, approval, provision, protection, authority and love of God forever.

3 | Home Reading and Questions

☐ **Isaiah 61:10**

In the Bible, clothing is often used as a metaphor to describe the reality of a person's heart.

I: Imagine what it would feel like in your heart, to be completely embraced by the Father and clothed with the garment of salvation (saving love).

Q: What does it mean to be saved by God? Saved from what?

Q: What would it be like to be lavished with God's love?

☐ **1 John 4:7-14**

I: Imagine a God, who is love. Imagine how this God thinks. How He feels. Imagine a God who can only love. Imagine this love, bursting forth in creative power at the beginning of time. Imagine this God of love, releasing His love into creation as He formed and created you.

Q: What does it mean for God to create me in love?

Q: Do I really love other people?

Q: What is love?

Q: Can God ever not love?

☐ **Matthew 5:38-48**
Q: What is Jesus revealing about God in this passage?

Q: Why does God make it rain and shine on both the righteous and the unrighteous people?

Q: What does it mean for me to love my enemies?

☐ **John 13:1-17**
I: Imagine being among the disciples. Imagine having hot, dusty, sweaty feet. Imagine Jesus, taking a towel and washing your feet.

Q: Why did Jesus wash His disciples' feet?

Q: What does Jesus reveal about God in this passage?

Q: Why did Jesus call His followers to serve each other?

☐ **Prayer** God, I'd like more love in my life. If you really are love, can you please show me your love? Can you please help me to receive your love?

☐ **John 7 - John 9**
Write down your questions here:

☐ Experiences with God

Write down your some of your own prayers, discoveries, questions and experiences.

4 | Jesus and the Father

John 14:1-11

[1]"Let not your hearts be troubled. Believe in God; believe also in me. [2]In my Father's house are many rooms. If it were not so, would I have told you that I go to prepare a place for you? [3]And if I go and prepare a place for you, I will come again and will take you to myself, that where I am you may be also. [4]And you know the way to where I am going." [5]Thomas said to him, "Lord, we do not know where you are going. How can we know the way?" [6]Jesus said to him, "I am the way, and the truth, and the life. No one comes to the Father except through me. [7]If you had known me, you would have known my Father also. From now on you do know him and have seen him."

[8]Philip said to him, "Lord, show us the Father, and it is enough for us." [9]Jesus said to him, "Have I been with you so long, and you still do not know me, Philip? Whoever has seen me has seen the Father. How can you say, 'Show us the Father'? [10]Do you not believe that I am in the Father and the Father is in me? The words that I say to you I do not speak on my own authority, but the Father who dwells in me does his works. [11]Believe me that I am in the Father and the Father is in me, or else believe on account of the works themselves."

Q: Who is the Father?

Q: What does Jesus mean when He says "If you had known me, you would have known my Father also" and "whoever has seen me has seen the Father"?

Father + Son = 1

John 10:22-33

[22]At that time the Feast of Dedication took place at Jerusalem. It was winter, [23]and Jesus was walking in the temple, in the colonnade of Solomon. [24]So the Jews gathered around him and said to him, "How long will you keep us in suspense? If you are the Christ, tell us plainly." [25]Jesus answered them, "I told you, and you do not believe. The works that I do in my Father's name bear witness about me, [26]but you do not believe because you are not among my sheep. [27]My sheep hear my voice, and I know them, and they follow me. [28]I give them eternal life, and they will never perish, and no one will snatch them out of my hand. [29]My Father, who has given them to me, is greater than all, and no one is able to snatch them out of the Father's hand. [30]I and the Father are one."

[31]The Jews picked up stones again to stone him. [32]Jesus answered them, "I have shown you many good works from the Father; for which of them are you going to stone me?" [33]The Jews answered him, "It is not for a good work that we are going to stone you but for blasphemy, because you, being a man, make yourself God."

Q: What does Jesus mean when He says "I and the Father are one"?

Q: Why did the Jews want to kill Jesus?

" The Jews wanted to kill Jesus because He insisted that He was God. He was (and is) the only source of eternal life. He and the Father are One. It was not long before Jesus was killed because of His claim to be God.

Q: At the time, claiming to be God was a death sentence. If Jesus was just a religious teacher and He knew that He was not actually God, why would He risk death for a lie?

"
So we are left with only two valid perspectives on Jesus:
1. Jesus really is God and everything He said was true; or
2. He was insane to the point of dying for a delusion, and we cannot trust anything He said.

Q: Is this fair that there are only two positions that we can have on Jesus? Or are there other perspectives?

Son of God

Matthew 16:13-17
[13]Now when Jesus came into the district of Caesarea Philippi, he asked his disciples, "Who do people say that the Son of Man is?" [14]And they said, "Some say John the Baptist, others say Elijah, and others Jeremiah or one of the prophets." [15]He said to them, "But who do you say that I am?" [16]Simon Peter replied, "You are the Christ, the Son of the living God." [17]And Jesus answered him, "Blessed are you, Simon Bar-Jonah! For flesh and blood has not revealed this to you, but my Father who is in heaven."

Q: What does it mean for Jesus to be the Christ, the Son of the living God?

God the Word with God

John 1: 1-5

[1]In the beginning was the Word, and the Word was with God, and the Word was God. [2]He was in the beginning with God. [3]All things were made through him, and without him was not any thing made that was made. [4]In him was life, and the life was the light of men. [5]The light shines in the darkness, and the darkness has not overcome it.

Q: How can 'the Word' be a *him?*

In this passage, John describes Jesus as the *Word of God.* The term *word* here is the Greek word *logos*, which means an expression or statement. It was used by Greek people at the time to refer to the divine but impersonal force, which governed the universe and gave all things life. A Jewish perspective was that the "Logos of the living God is the bond of everything, holding all things together…" Here John confirms that the logos is truly divine, and that the logos is the creative power of God that sustains and gives life to all things. Yet John goes a step beyond Greek thought by revealing that the divine logos is not an impersonal force but a person: the Eternal God in the person of Jesus Christ.

Read the passage again, replacing *Word* with *Jesus:*

John 1: 1-5

[1]In the beginning was Jesus, and Jesus was with God, and Jesus was God. [2]He was in the beginning with God. [3]All things were made through Jesus, and without him was not any thing made that was made. [4]In Jesus was life, and the life was the light of men. [5]The light [of Jesus] shines in the darkness, and the darkness has not overcome it.

Q: How can it be that at the beginning, Jesus was with God and at the same time Jesus was God?

Q: How can God be a person?

Q: Why did God become a person?

Only God with God

John 1: 14-18

[14] And the Word became flesh and dwelt among us, and we have seen his glory, glory as of the only Son from the Father, full of grace and truth. [15] (John bore witness about him, and cried out, "This was he of whom I said, 'He who comes after me ranks before me, because he was before me.'") [16] For from his fullness we have all received, grace upon grace. [17] For the law was given through Moses; grace and truth came through Jesus Christ. [18] No one has ever seen God; the only God, who is at the Father's side, he has made him known.

Q: Who is "the only God who is at the Father's side"?

Q: What has He done?

> The whole Bible centers around Jesus. He reveals the Father to us, not because He has had a special insight or revelation of God, but because He is God. He and the Father are One. When we read of the life of Jesus, we see the life of God being expressed on earth. When we read His teachings, we get insight into the nature of God. Jesus is the light of revelation because He is the Light of God. The Bible simply says that Jesus is God.

Q: So who do you say Jesus is?

Summary

> Through His life and His teachings, Jesus left no middle ground to stand on. Either we accept that everything He said was true, or we deny it all. By willingly dying for calling Himself God, Jesus Himself denies us the option of believing that He was just a good teacher and no more. So we simply cannot pick and choose which of His teachings we agree with. It is a case of all or nothing.

If we choose to believe that Jesus is God then we also need to think about what that means for our lives and how we should respond to Him. What does Jesus teach us about answering His call? What does He show us about what it means to follow Him?

4 | Home Reading and Questions

☐ **Colossians 1:15-20**
I: Imagine Jesus having the fullness of God dwelling within Him, cloaked in humility.

Q: All things were created through Jesus and for Him. So what does that mean for me to be created *for* Jesus?

Q: If Jesus created everything, what could I possibly give back to Him? What could I give Jesus that He doesn't already have?

Q: Do I have real peace with God?

☐ **Philippians 2:1-11**
I: Imagine Jesus existing in the form of God. Imagine Him emptying Himself and becoming a man. Imagine the Creator of the universe, humbling Himself to become a servant and to suffer death for us.

Q: Is it possible to do "nothing from selfishness"? Why?

Q: What attitude did Jesus have when He became a man?

Q: How can I have that same attitude?

☐ **Acts17:22-28**
Q: Is God far from me?

Q: What does it mean for me to "live and move and have my being" in God?

Q: If God created me then can I call myself a child of God?

☐ **Prayer** Dear God, if you're real, can you please reveal yourself to me and help me to know what it means to follow you.

☐ **John 10 - John 12**
Write down your questions here:

☐ **Experiences with God**

Write down your some of your own prayers, discoveries, questions and experiences.

5 | Jesus the Reality

One Way

John 14:6
Jesus said to him, "I am the way, and the truth, and the life. No one comes to the Father except through me."

Q: Why is Jesus the only way to God?

Q: What does it mean for Jesus to be the truth?

" In early Greek culture, the Greek word *aletheia* (truth) was used to express **reality** as opposed to fantasy or illusion. Truth is reality. So when Jesus says "I am the Truth", He is saying that He is Reality—the ultimate Reality.

Q: What does it mean for Jesus to be Reality?

Q: If Jesus is Reality, what does it mean to live apart from Jesus?

Q: What does it mean to live in a fantasy?

Q: In the story of the Father's love, did the younger son live in the reality or fantasy?

Q: Was the fantasy enjoyable?

Q: Do we want to live in reality?

Word of Reality

John 17:13-17 – Jesus prays to the Father

[13] "But now I am coming to you, and these things I speak in the world, that they may have my joy fulfilled in themselves. [14] I have given them your word, and the world has hated them because they are not of the world, just as I am not of the world. [15] I do not ask that you take them out of the world, but that you keep them from the evil one. [16] They are not of the world, just as I am not of the world. [17] Sanctify them in the truth; your word is truth."

❝ The word *sanctify* means to set apart and make pure. So Jesus is praying that God would set His people apart and purify them by His word of truth.

Q: God's word is truth and reality. What does that tell us about the Bible?

Spirit of Reality

John 14:16-17
[16] And I will ask the Father, and he will give you another Helper, to be with you forever, [17] even the Spirit of truth, whom the world cannot receive, because it neither sees him nor knows him. You know him, for he dwells with you and will be in you.

John 16:13
[13] When the Spirit of truth comes, he will guide you into all the truth, for he will not speak on his own authority, but whatever he hears he will speak, and he will declare to you the things that are to come.

❝ In terms of truth and reality, these verses show that Jesus has promised to give us the Spirit of Reality who will help us and guide us into reality. He will live within us and speak whatever God tells Him, and show us what He is leading us into. In this way, God does not leave us just with His word telling us about the truth. He gives us His Spirit to help us to experience the reality of His truth.

Q: What's the difference between learning about God's love and experiencing the reality of His love?

Q: Do we want to experience the reality of God's love?

Romans 5:1-5

[1] Therefore, since we have been justified by faith, we have peace with God through our Lord Jesus Christ. [2] Through him we have also obtained access by faith into this grace in which we stand, and we rejoice in hope of the glory of God. [3] Not only that, but we rejoice in our sufferings, knowing that suffering produces endurance, [4] and endurance produces character, and character produces hope, [5] and hope does not put us to shame, because God's love has been poured into our hearts through the Holy Spirit who has been given to us.

Q: We can learn about God's love in the Bible, but we can only experience His love poured into our hearts through His Holy Spirit. So if we can only receive the love of God through the Holy Spirit then who or what is the Spirit?

" Jesus has lots of different names. He is called Immanuel, the Prince of Peace, the Alpha and Omega, the Son of Man etc. Likewise, the Holy Spirit is also known by different names such as the Spirit of Truth, the Spirit of God, and the Spirit of Jesus.

As humans, we have been created with a heart, soul, mind and body. Our body is a container for our material life (like our blood, bones, muscles and organs). Our mind is a container for our thoughts. And our heart (spiritual not physical) is a container for our spirit, which is the substance of our inner nature and character. When we receive the Holy Spirit, He fills our hearts with His presence and He redefines our inner nature and character. It's like our heart becomes a shared space with the Spirit of Jesus. When the Spirit of Jesus dwells within us, we automatically start to share in and experience the reality of Jesus. Because His own Spirit is within us, Jesus shares His love with us and pours it out into our hearts. His love then changes us. It changes our nature and character. It changes the way we think, how we feel, our intentions and motivations, and ultimately our actions.

Imagining the Impossible

1 Corinthians 2:9-16

[9]"But, as it is written— What no eye has seen, nor ear heard, nor the heart of man imagined, what God has prepared for those who love him"— [10]these things God has revealed to us through the Spirit. For the Spirit searches everything, even the depths of God. [11]For who knows a person's thoughts except the spirit of that person, which is in him? So also no one comprehends the thoughts of God except the Spirit of God. [12]Now we have received not the spirit of the world, but the Spirit who is from God, that we might understand the things freely given us by God. [13]And we impart this in words not taught by human wisdom but taught by the Spirit, interpreting spiritual truths to those who are spiritual.

[14]The natural person does not accept the things of the Spirit of God, for they are folly to him, and he is not able to understand them because they are spiritually discerned. [15]The spiritual person judges all things, but is himself to be judged by no one. [16]"For who has understood the mind of the Lord so as to instruct him?" But we have the mind of Christ.

Q: What has God prepared for those who love Him?

Q: Why does God give us His Spirit?

" Just as God gives us His Spirit so that He can share His heart with us, so He also gives us His Spirit so that He can share His mind with us. No one can possibly know the thoughts of God except for the Spirit of God. So God gives us His Spirit to share His thoughts with us and reveal the awesome things that God has prepared for us. These things are our inheritance in Jesus: they are the blessings, gifts, love, power and times of transformation that we experience as we take possession of our spiritual inheritance.

Ephesians 3:20-21
²⁰Now to him who is able to do far more abundantly than all that we ask or think, according to the power at work within us, ²¹to him be glory in the church and in Christ Jesus throughout all generations, forever and ever. Amen.

Q: What can God do for us?

Summary

" Truth is reality and Jesus is the ultimate truth. Everything that is real flows from the reality of Jesus. He is life and gives life. Jesus is the centre, source and sustainer of reality.

To live more in the truth is to live in deeper connection and relationship with Jesus. It is to experience more of the life, love, nature, presence and power of Jesus Christ.

The word of God describes the reality that is found in Jesus. Because God's word is truth, the experiences we have of God will always be consistent with the word. It is the standard of reality. It is the foundation for our experience.

To lead us into reality, God has given us His Spirit. The Spirit of God takes the truth of the word and leads us into the personal experience of that truth. Through His Spirit, Jesus also shares His heart and His mind with us. When the Spirit of Jesus dwells within us, He pours out the love of God into us and shares the thoughts of God with us.

5 | Home Reading and Questions

☐ **Psalm 139:17-18**

This is a song, written by King David of Israel.

Q: How did David know the thoughts of God?

Q: Why were God's thoughts so precious to David?

Q: Would God want to share His thoughts with me?

I: Imagine a God of love whose thoughts are so vast they are impossible to count. Imagine Him thinking about you. Imagine Him sharing some of His thoughts with you.

☐ **Ephesians 3:14-21**

I: Imagine a love that surpasses knowledge. Imagine being the object of that love.

Q: What does it mean to be filled with God?

Q: Can God really do abundantly more than I could ask or think?

Q: What is the limit of my imagination? If I could ask God for anything, what would I ask for?

☐ **Romans 8:28-30**
Q: How can God make everything work out for good?

Q: Would God want to make everything in my life work out for good?

Q: What does it mean to be conformed to the image of God's Son?

☐ **Prayer** God, if you are real, I'd like to know what you have prepared for me. Please share your thoughts with me and show me something of the life you'd like to give me.

☐ John 13 - John 15
Write down your questions here:

☐ **Experiences with God**

Write down your some of your own prayers, discoveries, questions and experiences.

6 | Image of God

Colossians 1:15-20

[15] He [Jesus] is the image of the invisible God, the firstborn of all creation. [16] For by him all things were created, in heaven and on earth, visible and invisible, whether thrones or dominions or rulers or authorities—all things were created through him and for him. [17] And he is before all things, and in him all things hold together.

Q: What is an image?

Q: What does it mean for Jesus to be the image of God?

Q: How can Jesus be God, but also be the image of God? Isn't an image a copy?

Created in His Image

Genesis 1:26

[26] Then God said, "Let us make man in our image, after our likeness. And let them have dominion over the fish of the sea and over the birds of the heavens and over the livestock and over all the earth and over every creeping thing that creeps on the earth."

Q: Who does "us" refer to?

Q: What was God's design for people?

Q: If Jesus is the image of God then what does it mean to be designed in His image?

" When God created people, He did not make a copy of His nature of love and place it in the heart of man. Instead He created people to exist in unity with Him, sharing the heart and nature of Jesus.

To separate the qualities of God's nature from Jesus Christ is like trying to separate the breath in our lungs from the air around us. We do not take a breath from the atmosphere and call it our own and then try to hold onto it forever. Rather we share the air around us, continually breathing it in and releasing it out. The air within us is united with the air around us.

In the same way, we do not receive love from God and then separate that love from Him by calling it our own. On the contrary, the presence of God's love in our hearts connects us to the Source. Like air, God's love is the basis of our unity with Him and it needs to continually flow back to Him. In this way, to be created in the image of God is not to be created just as a reflection of God, but to be created in unity with God. It is to have His nature alive within us, being expressed through our words and actions of love.

Q: What does it mean to live in unity with Jesus?

Q: So if we are all created in the image of God then is everyone living according to God's image?

Q: So why? What happened to the divine image in people?

An Image Lost

Romans 1:16-25

[16] For I am not ashamed of the gospel, for it is the power of God for salvation to everyone who believes, to the Jew first and also to the Greek. [17] For in it the righteousness of God is revealed from faith for faith, as it is written, "The righteous shall live by faith."

[18] For the wrath of God is revealed from heaven against all ungodliness and unrighteousness of men, who by their unrighteousness suppress the truth. [19] For what can be known about God is plain to them, because God has shown it to them. [20] For his invisible attributes, namely, his eternal power and divine nature, have been clearly perceived, ever since the creation of the world, in the things that have been made. So they are without excuse. [21] For although they knew God, they did not honor him as God or give thanks to him, but they became futile in their thinking, and their foolish hearts were darkened. [22] Claiming to be wise, they became fools, [23] and exchanged the glory of the immortal God for images resembling mortal man and birds and animals and creeping things.

[24] Therefore God gave them up in the lusts of their hearts to impurity, to the dishonoring of their bodies among themselves, [25] because they exchanged the truth about God for a lie and worshiped and served the creature rather than the Creator, who is blessed forever! Amen.

Q: What is this passage saying about the image of God in man?

Q: What impact did the choice to sin have on the identity of people?

> God's image is love and the opposite of love isn't hate. It's selfishness. When we traded the image of God for our own image, we began to live for ourselves rather than for God. We abandoned God's ways so we could make our own way. We did not want to be told who we were or what we should do. We wanted to be independent and answerable to no one. So we gave up God's design for our lives and created our own identity. We made ourselves our god.
>
> The big problem with this was that by rejecting the image of God, we rejected Jesus and broke our unity with Him. We disconnected from our Creator, which meant that we lost the power of His love within us and became enslaved to self. Without the love of God in our hearts, we weren't able to act according to God's image. We could try to be loving, but ultimately we were powerless to overcome our own selfishness and truly live in selfless love.

Q: In Romans 1:18, it says that God's wrath is revealed against all ungodliness and unrighteousness. What is unrighteousness and ungodliness? Why does God's intense anger burn towards unrighteousness and ungodliness?

According to the Bible, *righteousness* is the approval of God that comes from trusting in Him and expressing His love. It is acting *right* in God's sight because we possess and express His nature of pure love. To be *unrighteous* is to lack the love of God and to act against His love. Such action is also called *sin.* Sin covers all non-loving action, from the more serious acts such as murder, rape, adultery and abuse, to less violent acts such lying, stealing, manipulating and degrading others. Regardless of the nature of the act, all sin ultimately finds its source in selfishness. Selfishness, not hatred, is the true opposite of love. So regardless of what we do, we live in *unrighteousness, ungodliness* and *sin* simply when we live selfishly.

Light does not accommodate darkness. Instead, when we turn the lights on, the darkness disappears. In the same way, love cannot accommodate evil—love must overcome and destroy all sin, evil and selfishness. This is why the wrath of God burns against unrighteousness and ungodliness. God hates everything that opposes His love and His design for us.

Q: So where does that leave us? Does the anger of God burn against for following our selfish ways or does the love of God burn for us?

Summary

Jesus Christ is the image of God. The essence and nature and power of God are found in Jesus Christ. When God created people, He created us in His image and likeness. He designed us to live in a unity of love with Jesus Christ Himself.

So when God the Father created us, He created us through Jesus and specifically *for* Him. We were not created to be our own. Yet every single person throughout all history has chosen to go their own way. We have all denied the purpose of God for our lives and chosen self over love. When we chose to make our own way in life, we corrupted God's image within us. We traded His eternal love for temporal lust. We swapped truth for a lie and embraced fantasy over reality. We denied God and become self-conscious instead of God-conscious. The result was that we became enslaved to this thing called 'self'. Self ruled over us. It forced us to act upon our selfish passions and desires. Self became our god, and despite all the benefits and successes that putting self first brings in life, none of it can fill the void within our hearts. Every one of us has a need that can only be filled by one thing: the love of God.

6 | Home Reading and Questions

☐ **Hebrews 1:1-3**
Q: What does it mean for Jesus to be the radiance of God's glory?

Q: What does it mean for Jesus to be the exact representation (imprint/likeness) of God's nature?

Q: What does it mean for Jesus to uphold (or sustain) all things by His word?

☐ **Matthew 17:1-3**
I: Imagine being with Peter, James and John, and seeing Jesus reveal Himself. Imagine watching Jesus radiate God's glory, with His face shining like the sun, and His clothes white as light. Imagine God coming as a cloud of light, speaking of His love for Jesus and calling us to listen to Jesus.

Q: How could Jesus change Himself into light?

Q: What does it mean for Jesus to be the "light of life"? (see John 1)

Q: What would be my response if I saw Jesus reveal Himself as light?

Q: How would that change me?

☐ **Ephesians 4:17-24**

Q: What does it mean to be darkened in my understanding?

Q: What have I given myself up to?

Q: What is the old self? What is it like?

Q: What is the new self? What is it like?

Q: Who am I? Does my identity flow from my old self, my new self, or both?

Q: Who has God created me to be?

☐ **Prayer** Jesus, if you are light, could you please bring light to my life? Can you help me to see who you created me to be?

☐ **John 16 - John 17**
Write down your questions here:

☐ Experiences with God

Write down your some of your own prayers, discoveries, questions and experiences.

7 | Paying the Debt

Colossians 1:15-20

[15] He [Jesus] is the image of the invisible God, the firstborn of all creation. [16] For by him all things were created, in heaven and on earth, visible and invisible, whether thrones or dominions or rulers or authorities—all things were created through him and for him. [17] And he is before all things, and in him all things hold together.

Q: What does it mean for everything to be created for Jesus?

Q: What does it mean to be created as an expression of the Father's love for Jesus?

" God created people to live in His image as vessels of His love for Jesus. We were designed to be channels through which the love of God would always flow. Yet we all rejected God's image for our lives and chose selfishness over love. By living for self, we closed our hearts to God's love. Instead of being vessels of the Creator and His love, we became vessels of self, sin, brokenness and corruption.

Psalm 53:1-3

[1] The fool says in his heart, "There is no God."
    they are corrupt, doing abominable iniquity;
    there is none who does good.

² God looks down from heaven
   on the children of man
   to see if there are any who understand,
   who seek after God.
³ They have all fallen away;
   together they have become corrupt;
   there is none who does good,
   not even one.

Q: Has anyone ever lived their entire life in God's image?

Romans 6:20-23
²⁰ For when you were slaves of sin, you were free in regard to righteousness. ²¹ But what fruit were you getting at that time from the things of which you are now ashamed? For the end of those things is death. ²² But now that you have been set free from sin and have become slaves of God, the fruit you get leads to sanctification and its end, eternal life. ²³ For the wages of sin is death, but the free gift of God is eternal life in Christ Jesus our Lord.

Q: What does it mean "wages of sin"?

Sin as a Weighty Debt

" The Bible likens sin to a weight, a crime, and a debt. The weight of sin is the burden that we carry when we know in our hearts that we've done wrong. It is the weight of an ongoing spiritual death—of not being right with God and united with Him.

Sin is also like a crime because when we sin we break God's divine Law of Love. If we commit a crime in society, we are forced to accept the consequences. In the same way, when we sin, our actions mean that we are bound to suffer the sentence required by law for those actions. By acting selfishly we have broken God's law and we will have to face the inevitable sentence for our actions.

Finally, the Bible also likens sin to a debt that needs to be paid. As God's creation we have been made for Jesus and so we owe Him our lives—all our time, everything we are and have, it was all created to be an instrument of love for Jesus. We never had the right to abandon our purpose and take our lives away from Jesus. By going our own way, we stole our lives from God. When God created us, He invested such power and value in us that to waste our lives incurs an immeasurable debt with God. Every moment that we live for ourselves, every time we act selfishly, every time we sin, we incur an ever greater life-debt with God.

Psalm 40:5-9
⁵Why should I fear in times of trouble, when the iniquity of those who cheat me surrounds me,
⁶those who trust in their wealth and boast of the abundance of their riches?
⁷Truly no man can ransom another, or give to God the price of his life,
⁸for the ransom of their life is costly and can never suffice,
⁹that he should live on forever and never see the pit.

Q: What does it mean to ransom a life?

Q: What does the ransom purchase?

Q: Is there any way we can ransom our own lives?

Q: So how can we get right with God? How can the debt be paid?

Life-Debt Nailed

Colossians 2: 8-15

[8] See to it that no one takes you captive by philosophy and empty deceit, according to human tradition, according to the elemental spirits of the world, and not according to Christ. [9] For in him the whole fullness of deity dwells bodily, [10] and you have been filled in him, who is the head of all rule and authority. [11] In him also you were circumcised with a circumcision made without hands, by putting off the body of the flesh, by the circumcision of Christ, [12] having been buried with him in baptism, in which you were also raised with him through faith in the powerful working of God, who raised him from the dead. [13] And you, who were dead in your trespasses and the uncircumcision of your flesh, God made alive together with him, having forgiven us all our trespasses, [14] by canceling the record of debt that stood against us with its legal demands. This he set aside, nailing it to the cross. [15] He disarmed the rulers and authorities and put them to open shame, by triumphing over them in him.

Q: What is the record of debt that stood against us with all of its legal commands?

Q: What does it mean to have that debt cancelled?

Q: How was it cancelled out?

Q: What happened at the cross?

> We live in a world which offers us wealth, pleasure and entertainment as its highest rewards. We live in a world that exalts material success; in a world that denies a Creator and sacrifices the love of God on the altar of self. We live in a world that considers sin normal, even healthy. We live in a world which refuses to accept any moral standard, where lust reigns and love for others is redefined as tolerance.
>
> Because the voice of the world is constantly preaching to us, it is hard not to let it affect our thinking on sin. When so many people consider lying as a useful tool in life, it can be hard to see lying for what it is: a cold denial of the God of Truth and His image within us. In almost every aspect, we too easily fail to recognize the true nature of sin and the debt it incurs. We justify our choices to ourselves, but the truth remains: sin breaks the heart of our Creator, distorts His image within us, and incurs a life-debt that we cannot possibly hope to repay.

Forgiving the Debt

Matthew 18:23-35

[23] "Therefore the kingdom of heaven may be compared to a king who wished to settle accounts with his servants. [24] When he began to settle, one was brought to him who owed him ten thousand talents. [25] And since he could not pay, his master ordered him to be sold, with his wife and children and all that he had, and payment to be made. [26] So the servant fell on his knees, imploring him, 'Have patience with me, and I will pay you everything.' [27] And out of pity for him, the master of that servant released him and forgave him the debt. [28] But when that same servant went out, he found one of his fellow servants who owed him a hundred denarii, and seizing him, he began to choke him, saying, 'Pay what you owe.' [29] So his fellow servant fell down and pleaded with him, 'Have patience with me, and I will pay you.' [30] He refused and went and put him in prison until he should pay the debt. [31] When his fellow servants saw what had taken place, they were greatly distressed, and they went and reported to their master all that had taken place. [32] Then his master summoned him and said to him, 'You wicked servant! I forgave you all that debt because you pleaded with me. [33] And should not you have had mercy on your fellow servant, as I had mercy on you?' [34] And in anger his master delivered him to the jailers, until he should pay all his debt. [35] So also my heavenly Father will do to every one of you, if you do not forgive your brother from your heart."

It is interesting to note here that 10,000 talents would take 200,000 years for a laborer to earn. In other words, it was a debt that there was no possibility of paying off. In contrast, the debt of 200 denarii would have taken around four months for a laborer to earn. The high value speaks of the value that God has invested in our lives. As creations and channels of His love, each and every one of us is valued by God more than we could possibly comprehend.

Q: What does this say about the life-debt that we owe God?

Q: What does it say about the heart of God?

Q: What does God require of us when He forgives us?

Summary

" No one has ever lived their lives entirely for Jesus. Everyone has embraced sin and self, and rejected the image of God for their lives. Everyone has incurred a debt that no one could possibly repay. So we all chose to live in a fantasy, denying the debt of sin and instead justifying our actions to each other. But sin is too grave to embrace as a human weakness. Sin is an extreme offense to the God of Love. It is an ongoing denial of who God created us to be and the purpose and value He infused within us at our creation. All sin is theft—theft of the time and life that God created to be spent on loving Jesus and sharing His love with people.

Thankfully God sent Jesus to overcome our sin. Through Jesus' sacrifice, God forgives the debt of everyone who calls on His mercy and love. The record of our offenses against God is taken away by Jesus, erased entirely at the cross. Through Jesus, we can know the reality of being declared truly innocent of any sin before God.

7 | Home Reading and Questions

☐ **Matthew 18:1-9, Matthew 5:27-30**

Q: Why is it so bad to lead someone to sin?

Q: Why is sin so serious?

Q: How can we truly appreciate the gravity of sin?

Note that Jesus is not saying that we should literally and physically dismember ourselves to keep ourselves from sinning. As He says in Matthew 5, the source of sin is a corrupt heart, and entertaining the corrupt desires of the heart is as bad as actually committing them. Sin is a condition of the heart. In saying that we should cut off our hands and tear out our eyes, He is painting a graphic picture of the horror of sin. Jesus is trying to communicate how serious sin is and how damaging it is to us. If we cannot understand the serious nature of sin then we will never appreciate the real extent of the spiritual debt that our sin incurs.

☐ **Romans 3: 21-26**

Q: Why is it that everyone has sinned and fallen short of living the life that God designed?

Q: In what ways have I sinned?

Q: Would God forgive anyone at all? What about really evil people? Could they be forgiven as well?

Q: What does it mean to be justified by God?

☐ **Isaiah 55:6-7**
Q: What does it mean to seek God?

Q: What does it mean for me to forsake my unrighteous ways and thoughts?

Q: What will happen if I return to God?

Q: What does it mean for God to abundantly pardon me?

I: Imagine what it would feel like to have every sin washed away. Imagine what it would feel like to be totally forgiven and know that God fully loves and accepts you.

☐ **Luke 19:1-10**
Q: If I believe in Jesus, am I free from the consequences of my sin? If I have stolen from someone or lied to them, or mistreated someone, can I forget about all those things and pretend I didn't do them?

Q: What can I do for other people that would help to repair the damage my sin has caused for them?

☐ **Prayer** God, the Bible says that you will forgive anyone that asks for your mercy and love, even me. Can you help me to really believe that? I know there are people I need to forgive. Could you help me to forgive these people?

☐ John 18-20

Write down your questions here:

☐ **Experiences with God**

Write down your some of your own prayers, discoveries, questions and experiences.

8 | The Cross

Mark 15:1-39 (it's a long reading so share it around if needed)

[1] And as soon as it was morning, the chief priests held a consultation with the elders and scribes and the whole council. And they bound Jesus and led him away and delivered him over to Pilate. [2] And Pilate asked him, "Are you the King of the Jews?" And he answered him, "You have said so." [3] And the chief priests accused him of many things. [4] And Pilate again asked him, "Have you no answer to make? See how many charges they bring against you." [5] But Jesus made no further answer, so that Pilate was amazed.

[6] Now at the feast he used to release for them one prisoner for whom they asked. [7] And among the rebels in prison, who had committed murder in the insurrection, there was a man called Barabbas. [8] And the crowd came up and began to ask Pilate to do as he usually did for them. [9] And he answered them, saying, "Do you want me to release for you the King of the Jews?" [10] For he perceived that it was out of envy that the chief priests had delivered him up. [11] But the chief priests stirred up the crowd to have him release for them Barabbas instead. [12] And Pilate again said to them, "Then what shall I do with the man you call the King of the Jews?" [13] And they cried out again, "Crucify him." [14] And Pilate said to them, "Why, what evil has he done?" But they shouted all the more, "Crucify him." [15] So Pilate, wishing to satisfy the crowd, released for them Barabbas, and having scourged Jesus, he delivered him to be crucified.

[16] And the soldiers led him away inside the palace (that is, the governor's headquarters), and they called together the whole battalion. [17] And they clothed him in a purple cloak, and twisting together a crown of thorns, they put it on him. [18] And they began to salute him, "Hail, King of the Jews!" [19] And they were striking his head with a reed and spitting on him and kneeling down in homage to him. [20] And when they had mocked him, they stripped him of the purple cloak and put his own clothes on him. And they led him out to crucify him.

[21] And they compelled a passerby, Simon of Cyrene, who was coming in from the country, the father of Alexander and Rufus, to carry his cross. [22] And they brought him to the place called Golgotha (which means Place of a Skull). [23] And they offered him

wine mixed with myrrh, but he did not take it. [24] And they crucified him and divided his garments among them, casting lots for them, to decide what each should take. [25] And it was the third hour when they crucified him. [26] And the inscription of the charge against him read, "The King of the Jews." [27] And with him they crucified two robbers, one on his right and one on his left. [29] And those who passed by derided him, wagging their heads and saying, "Aha! You who would destroy the temple and rebuild it in three days, [30] save yourself, and come down from the cross!" [31] So also the chief priests with the scribes mocked him to one another, saying, "He saved others; he cannot save himself. [32] Let the Christ, the King of Israel, come down now from the cross that we may see and believe." Those who were crucified with him also reviled him.

[33] And when the sixth hour had come, there was darkness over the whole land until the ninth hour. [34] And at the ninth hour Jesus cried with a loud voice, "Eloi, Eloi, lema sabachthani?" which means, "My God, my God, why have you forsaken me?" [35] And some of the bystanders hearing it said, "Behold, he is calling Elijah." [36] And someone ran and filled a sponge with sour wine, put it on a reed and gave it to him to drink, saying, "Wait, let us see whether Elijah will come to take him down." [37] And Jesus uttered a loud cry and breathed his last. [38] And the curtain of the temple was torn in two, from top to bottom. [39] And when the centurion, who stood facing him, saw that in this way he breathed his last, he said, "Truly this man was the Son of God!"

Q: Had Jesus done anything evil, worthy of death?

Q: Why did the people want Jesus killed?

Q: Did Jesus die willingly?

Justified

Romans 5:6-11

6 For while we were still weak, at the right time Christ died for the ungodly. 7 For one will scarcely die for a righteous person—though perhaps for a good person one would dare even to die— 8 but God shows his love for us in that while we were still sinners, Christ died for us. 9 Since, therefore, we have now been justified by his blood, much more shall we be saved by him from the wrath of God. 10 For if while we were enemies we were reconciled to God by the death of his Son, much more, now that we are reconciled, shall we be saved by his life. 11 More than that, we also rejoice in God through our Lord Jesus Christ, through whom we have now received reconciliation.

Q: Why did Jesus die for us?

Q: What does justify mean?

Q: What does it mean to be reconciled to God?

Q: What does the sacrifice of Jesus mean for the debt that we owe God?

Not Guilty

Romans 8:1-8

¹There is therefore now no condemnation for those who are in Christ Jesus. ² For the law of the Spirit of life has set you free in Christ Jesus from the law of sin and death. ³ For God has done what the law, weakened by the flesh, could not do. By sending his own Son in the likeness of sinful flesh and for sin, he condemned sin in the flesh, ⁴ in order that the righteous requirement of the law might be fulfilled in us, who walk not according to the flesh but according to the Spirit.

" This can be a bit of a tricky passage to understand at first. The term "law" here refers to the standard of behavior that defines what it means to be righteous. It tells us which actions are good and which are evil. Just like the law of gravity describes the force that pulls us towards the earth, the moral law also describes the reality that *all sin leads to death.* It is inevitable. According to God's moral law, death is the inescapable consequence of sin, and it is as sure as any of His natural laws. The outcome is certain.

But simply knowing that sin leads to death and having a set of rules and commands that define righteous behavior doesn't actually help us to overcome our sin or selfishness. It simply tells us that we are sinners and that we are going to die apart from God. So instead of helping us, knowing all the rules just leaves us feeling overwhelmed and helpless to live righteously before God.

Condemnation is a death sentence. As long as we live in sin, we are living under a death sentence of separation from God. But, recognizing our helplessness, God sent Jesus to come as a person and to take our sin and die. Through His death, Jesus satisfied the law which stated that all sin must lead to death. He fulfilled the law and in doing so, He condemned sin itself. He died for us so that we won't be separated from God, now or ever for all eternity. He died to bring us back into unity with God. This is why there is no condemnation for those who are in Christ Jesus. There can't possibly be any condemnation for believers in Jesus because He has already died for our sin. Our sentence has already been served. The judgment has been already passed and executed through the sacrifice of Jesus Christ.

2 Corinthians 5:17-21

[17] Therefore, if anyone is in Christ, he is a new creation. The old has passed away; behold, the new has come. [18] All this is from God, who through Christ reconciled us to himself and gave us the ministry of reconciliation; [19] that is, in Christ God was reconciling the world to himself, not counting their trespasses against them, and entrusting to us the message of reconciliation. [20] Therefore, we are ambassadors for Christ, God making his appeal through us. We implore you on behalf of Christ, be reconciled to God. [21] For our sake he made him to be sin who knew no sin, so that in him we might become the righteousness of God.

Q: What is reconciliation?

Q: What does it mean that Jesus became sin?

Q: So if Jesus became sin for us, what happened to our sin when Jesus died?

Prophecy of the Lamb (if time allows)

" Around 700 years before Jesus came, God spoke to a prophet called Isaiah about Jesus.
He had already revealed Jesus' birth to Isaiah. Now God spoke of His sacrificial death.

Isaiah 53

Who has believed what he has heard from us?

  And to whom has the arm of the Lord been revealed?

2 For he grew up before him like a young plant,

  and like a root out of dry ground;

  he had no form or majesty that we should look at him,

  and no beauty that we should desire him.

3 He was despised and rejected by men;

  a man of sorrows, and acquainted with grief;

  and as one from whom men hide their faces

  he was despised, and we esteemed him not.

4 Surely he has borne our griefs

  and carried our sorrows;

  yet we esteemed him stricken,

  smitten by God, and afflicted.

5 But he was pierced for our transgressions;

  he was crushed for our iniquities;

  upon him was the chastisement that brought us peace,

  and with his wounds we are healed.

6 All we like sheep have gone astray;

  we have turned—every one—to his own way;

  and the Lord has laid on him

  the iniquity of us all.

7 He was oppressed, and he was afflicted,

  yet he opened not his mouth;

  like a lamb that is led to the slaughter,

  and like a sheep that before its shearers is silent,

  so he opened not his mouth.

8 By oppression and judgment he was taken away;
   and as for his generation, who considered
   that he was cut off out of the land of the living,
   stricken for the transgression of my people?
9 And they made his grave with the wicked
   and with a rich man in his death,
   although he had done no violence,
   and there was no deceit in his mouth.
10 Yet it was the will of the Lord to crush him;
   he has put him to grief;
   when his soul makes an offering for guilt,
   he shall see his offspring; he shall prolong his days;
   the will of the Lord shall prosper in his hand.
11 Out of the anguish of his soul he shall see and be satisfied;
   by his knowledge shall the righteous one, my servant,
   make many to be accounted righteous,
   and he shall bear their iniquities.
12 Therefore I will divide him a portion with the many,
   and he shall divide the spoil with the strong,
   because he poured out his soul to death
   and was numbered with the transgressors;
   yet he bore the sin of many,
   and makes intercession for the transgressors.

Q: What insights does the prophecy give us into the death of Jesus?

Summary

God created us in His image, through Jesus and for Him. But like wandering sheep, we all went astray. We chose the way of selfishness and sin and strayed from our identity and purpose in life. We stole our lives away from Jesus. And in doing so, we took on a debt that was impossible to pay.

But the God of love had a plan for our redemption. He sent His Son Jesus, who was and is God, to be the sacrifice for our sins. Jesus was entirely innocent of all sin. He had done no violence, and was not selfish or sinful in any way. This made Him the only one who could possibly act as a sacrifice for sin. So Jesus took our punishment. He became sin for us. He was falsely accused, unjustly condemned, and cruelly crucified. He suffered a painful and humiliating execution, which is what our sin demands. Through His death, our sin was completely taken away. His sacrifice took away our corruption and completely paid our life-debt to God. In Christ we can be free from the bondage of sin and restored back into relationship with God.

8 | Home Reading and Questions

☐ **Matthew 27:11-54**

I: Imagine being in the court, listening to Pilate talking to Jesus. Imagine seeing His trial. Imagine watching Him being beaten, mocked and finally crucified. Imagine seeing Jesus on the cross, watching Him bleed. Imagine hearing Jesus cry out. Imagine Him looking at you before closing His eyes and dying.

Q: Did Jesus sound like He was sane when He talked with Pilate?

Q: Why did Pilate find no guilt in Jesus?

Q: Why did Jesus choose to suffer such humiliation and pain?

Q: Did Jesus really die for me? If not, why else would He choose to die? If so, what does that mean for me?

☐ **Psalm 22:1-24**

This Psalm was written by King David of Israel around 1000 years before Jesus'
crucifixion.

I: Imagine the intensity of feeling as Jesus' life was poured out like water.

Q: How does this Psalm parallel Jesus' crucifixion?

Q: What emotion must Jesus have felt at the cross?

Q: Did God come through and deliver Him?

☐ **John 10:1-18**

Q: What is a good shepherd like?

Q: Did Jesus lay down His life at the cross willingly?

Q: Why?

☐ **Psalm 23**
Q: What does God promise me through this Psalm?

Q: What would it be like to know that I will never lack anything I need?

Q: What would it feel like for God to restore my soul?

Q: What would it be like to have goodness and love following me wherever I go?

☐ **Prayer** Jesus, did you really die for my sin? If so, why? Why would you die for me? Please show me what happened on the cross and how it can change my life.

☐ **John 21 – Acts 1**
Write down your questions here:

☐ **Experiences with God**
Write down your some of your own prayers, discoveries, questions and experiences.

9 | Resurrection Life

" The story of God's redemption doesn't end with the death of Jesus. Dying for our sin was only half the solution. In order for Jesus to complete His mission, He had to defeat both sin *and* death. So let's see how He does it.

Mark 8:27-31

[27] And Jesus went on with his disciples to the villages of Caesarea Philippi. And on the way he asked his disciples, "Who do people say that I am?" [28] And they told him, "John the Baptist; and others say, Elijah; and others, one of the prophets." [29] And he asked them, "But who do you say that I am?" Peter answered him, "You are the Christ." [30] And he strictly charged them to tell no one about him.

[31] And he began to teach them that the Son of Man must suffer many things and be rejected by the elders and the chief priests and the scribes and be killed, and after three days rise again.

Q: Why would Jesus teach that He was going to suffer and die and rise again?

Matthew 27:57-28:20 (it's a long passage, so share the reading around the group)

[57] When it was evening, there came a rich man from Arimathea, named Joseph, who also was a disciple of Jesus. [58] He went to Pilate and asked for the body of Jesus. Then Pilate ordered it to be given to him. [59] And Joseph took the body and wrapped it in a clean linen shroud [60] and laid it in his own new tomb, which he had cut in the rock. And he rolled a great stone to the entrance of the tomb and went away. [61] Mary Magdalene and the other Mary were there, sitting opposite the tomb.

[62] The next day, that is, after the day of Preparation, the chief priests and the Pharisees gathered before Pilate [63] and said, "Sir, we remember how that impostor said, while he was still alive, 'After three days I will rise.' [64] Therefore order the tomb

to be made secure until the third day, lest his disciples go and steal him away and tell the people, 'He has risen from the dead,' and the last fraud will be worse than the first." ⁶⁵ Pilate said to them, "You have a guard of soldiers. Go, make it as secure as you can." ⁶⁶ So they went and made the tomb secure by sealing the stone and setting a guard.

²⁸:¹ Now after the Sabbath, toward the dawn of the first day of the week, Mary Magdalene and the other Mary went to see the tomb. ² And behold, there was a great earthquake, for an angel of the Lord descended from heaven and came and rolled back the stone and sat on it. ³ His appearance was like lightning, and his clothing white as snow. ⁴ And for fear of him the guards trembled and became like dead men. ⁵ But the angel said to the women, "Do not be afraid, for I know that you seek Jesus who was crucified. ⁶ He is not here, for he has risen, as he said. Come, see the place where he lay. ⁷ Then go quickly and tell his disciples that he has risen from the dead, and behold, he is going before you to Galilee; there you will see him. See, I have told you." ⁸ So they departed quickly from the tomb with fear and great joy, and ran to tell his disciples. ⁹ And behold, Jesus met them and said, "Greetings!" And they came up and took hold of his feet and worshiped him. ¹⁰ Then Jesus said to them, "Do not be afraid; go and tell my brothers to go to Galilee, and there they will see me."

¹¹ While they were going, behold, some of the guard went into the city and told the chief priests all that had taken place. ¹² And when they had assembled with the elders and taken counsel, they gave a sufficient sum of money to the soldiers ¹³ and said, "Tell people, 'His disciples came by night and stole him away while we were asleep.' ¹⁴ And if this comes to the governor's ears, we will satisfy him and keep you out of trouble." ¹⁵ So they took the money and did as they were directed. And this story has been spread among the Jews to this day.

¹⁶ Now the eleven disciples went to Galilee, to the mountain to which Jesus had directed them. ¹⁷ And when they saw him they worshiped him, but some doubted. ¹⁸ And Jesus came and said to them, "All authority in heaven and on earth has been given to me. ¹⁹ Go therefore and make disciples of all nations, baptizing them in the name of the Father and of the Son and of the Holy Spirit, ²⁰ teaching them to observe all that I have commanded you. And behold, I am with you always, to the end of the age."

Q: Was Jesus really raised from the dead? How is that even possible?

Q: Jesus said He would rise again after His execution (*Mark 8:31, Luke 9:22*). What would it mean if Jesus didn't actually rise again?

Q: Is it more likely that Jesus was raised from dead by the power of God, or that He faked His resurrection?

Q: Why is the resurrection important?

Q: How important is it to believe in the resurrection if we want to follow Jesus?

Q: So what does it mean to experience the cross and the resurrection in our lives?

Immersed into Death and Life

Romans 6:1-4

¹ What shall we say then? Are we to continue in sin that grace may abound? ² By no means! How can we who died to sin still live in it? ³ Do you not know that all of us who have been baptized into Christ Jesus were baptized into his death? ⁴ We were buried therefore with him by baptism into death, in order that, just as Christ was raised from the dead by the glory of the Father, we too might walk in newness of life.

Q: What does it mean to be baptized (immersed) into the death of Jesus?

Q: What does it mean to walk in "newness of life"?

United with Christ

Romans 6:5-11

⁵ For if we have been united with him in a death like his, we shall certainly be united with him in a resurrection like his. ⁶ We know that our old self was crucified with him in order that the body of sin might be brought to nothing, so that we would no longer be enslaved to sin. ⁷ For one who has died has been set free from sin. ⁸ Now if we have died with Christ, we believe that we will also live with him. ⁹ We know that Christ, being raised from the dead, will never die again; death no longer has dominion over him. ¹⁰ For the death he died he died to sin, once for all, but the life he lives he lives to God. ¹¹ So you also must consider yourselves dead to sin and alive to God in Christ Jesus.

Q: Is resurrection life something we can experience now or is it for later, after we physically die?

Q: What does it mean for the "old self" to be crucified with Christ? What is the old self?

The Old Self

Colossians 3:1-11

[1] If then you have been raised with Christ, seek the things that are above, where Christ is, seated at the right hand of God. [2] Set your minds on things that are above, not on things that are on earth. [3] For you have died, and your life is hidden with Christ in God. [4] When Christ who is your life appears, then you also will appear with him in glory.

[5] Put to death therefore what is earthly in you: sexual immorality, impurity, passion, evil desire, and covetousness, which is idolatry. [6] On account of these the wrath of God is coming. [7] In these you too once walked, when you were living in them. [8] But now you must put them all away: anger, wrath, malice, slander, and obscene talk from your mouth. [9] Do not lie to one another, seeing that you have put off the old self with its practices [10] and have put on the new self, which is being renewed in knowledge after the image of its creator. [11] Here there is not Greek and Jew, circumcised and uncircumcised, barbarian, Scythian, slave, free; but Christ is all, and in all.

" The "old self" is our old identity. It is the corrupt nature within our hearts that compels us to sin. It is all the darkness and selfishness within us that distorts God's image and design for our lives. In Scripture, the old self is also simply called *the flesh*.

The "new self" is our new identity in union with Jesus. It is who we truly are: people created in the image of God, who live in His love and power. Through the cross, Jesus released His power to bring the old self to death, and through His resurrection He released His power to bring us into the reality of our new identity in His image.

Q: What would it be like for the "old self" to be crucified with Christ?

Q: How can this happen?

Q: What would our new self look like? How would it feel?

" Long before He died, Jesus told His disciples that it was essential that He suffer, die and rise again. The disciples didn't understand it at the time, but everything Jesus said came to pass. He was arrested, tortured, abused and humiliated. Because of His love, the Son of God, for whom all creation was made, willingly let Himself be hung on a cross, exposed, shamed and mocked by His own creation. Yet far from being a defeat, Jesus' unjust execution was all a part of God's plan to free us from all sin. The cross was a resounding victory. Sin was put to death.

Having conquered sin, Jesus then overcame death itself. The Spirit of God raised Him back to life and now Jesus lives forever and cannot ever die. Now he invites us to be united with Him in his death and resurrection. Jesus calls us to let Him crucify our old life so that we can experience a new life through the power of His resurrection.

9 | Home Reading and Questions

☐ **1 Corinthians 15:1-19**
Q: How many people did Jesus appear to after His resurrection?

Q: Why is Jesus' resurrection so important?

I: Imagine being among all the people who saw Jesus. Imagine that you watched Him die, and now you see Him alive. Imagine Him looking through the crowd and locking eyes with you.

☐ **1 Peter 2:21-25**
Q: Who did Jesus suffer for?

Q: Why did Jesus bear our sins on the cross?

Q: How are we healed by Jesus' wounds?

Q: Am I straying away, or am I returning to the Shepherd and Guardian of my soul?

□ **Philippians 3:7-11**
Q: What would it be like to know the power of Jesus' resurrection?

Q: What would it be like to be conformed to His death?

Q: Do I want my old life to be crucified with Jesus?

Q: Do I want a new life with Jesus?

Q: What would my new life with Jesus look like?

☐ **Prayer** Jesus, if you're alive now, please help me to believe. Help me to really believe that you died and rose again, so that I could die with you and rise with you. Help me to really want this.

☐ **Acts 2-3**
Write down your questions here:

☐ **Experiences with God**

Write down your some of your own prayers, discoveries, questions and experiences.

10 | Grace through Faith

" Jesus died and was raised again for us. He died to take away our sin, and He was raised again so that we might have eternal life—an unending life in His image, in union with Him. In this study we will look at how we receive this new life.

Acts 2:22-41 (can skip ahead to verse 36 if you like)

[22] "Men of Israel, hear these words: Jesus of Nazareth, a man attested to you by God with mighty works and wonders and signs that God did through him in your midst, as you yourselves know— [23] this Jesus, delivered up according to the definite plan and foreknowledge of God, you crucified and killed by the hands of lawless men. [24] God raised him up, loosing the pangs of death, because it was not possible for him to be held by it. [25] For David says concerning him,

> "'I saw the Lord always before me,
> for he is at my right hand that I may not be shaken;
> [26] therefore my heart was glad, and my tongue rejoiced;
> my flesh also will dwell in hope.
> [27] For you will not abandon my soul to Hades,
> or let your Holy One see corruption.
> [28] You have made known to me the paths of life;
> you will make me full of gladness with your presence.'

[29] "Brothers, I may say to you with confidence about the patriarch David that he both died and was buried, and his tomb is with us to this day. [30] Being therefore a prophet, and knowing that God had sworn with an oath to him that he would set one of his descendants on his throne, [31] he foresaw and spoke about the resurrection of the Christ, that he was not abandoned to Hades, nor did his flesh see corruption. [32] This Jesus God raised up, and of that we all are witnesses. [33] Being therefore exalted at the right hand of God, and having received from the Father the promise of the Holy Spirit,

he has poured out this that you yourselves are seeing and hearing. [34] For David did not ascend into the heavens, but he himself says,

> "'The Lord said to my Lord,
> "Sit at my right hand,
> [35] until I make your enemies your footstool."'

[36] Let all the house of Israel therefore know for certain that God has made him both Lord and Christ, this Jesus whom you crucified."

[37] Now when they heard this they were cut to the heart, and said to Peter and the rest of the apostles, "Brothers, what shall we do?" [38] And Peter said to them, "Repent and be baptized every one of you in the name of Jesus Christ for the forgiveness of your sins, and you will receive the gift of the Holy Spirit. [39] For the promise is for you and for your children and for all who are far off, everyone whom the Lord our God calls to himself." [40] And with many other words he bore witness and continued to exhort them, saying, "Save yourselves from this crooked generation." [41] So those who received his word were baptized, and there were added that day about three thousand souls.

Q: What does it mean to repent for the forgiveness of sins?

" In terms of receiving the power of the cross, we repent when we turn to God and seek Him to crucify our old life. We repent when we disown our old identity and seek God for His image. Repentance is giving up on going our own way in life and seeking God to show us His way. If we repent and turn to God, our forgiveness is guaranteed. God will completely forgive every wrong, every sin, and every act of selfishness forever. Our spiritual state will be totally clean and we will be completely innocent before God.

Baptism

Q: Why did the people get baptized when they believed?

" Water baptism is an expression of faith and repentance. It is a sign that we believe God and that we have given our lives back to Him. When we get baptized in water, we make the statement that we are uniting ourselves with Jesus, and we are living for Him. We are giving our old life over to be crucified with Him, and we are receiving His gift of new life. Without faith, being immersed or baptized in water achieves nothing. But with faith, it becomes a powerful expression of our new life with Jesus.

When people fall in love and commit to living their lives together, they get married. They publically declare their love and invite their friends to their wedding to celebrate their new life together. In many ways, baptism is like the wedding celebration. It is a public declaration of our love for God and a chance for others to celebrate our new life with us.

Forgiveness through the Blood

1 John 1:5-10

⁵ This is the message we have heard from him and proclaim to you, that God is light, and in him is no darkness at all. ⁶ If we say we have fellowship with him while we walk in darkness, we lie and do not practice the truth. ⁷ But if we walk in the light, as he is in the light, we have fellowship with one another, and the blood of Jesus his Son cleanses us from all sin. ⁸ If we say we have no sin, we deceive ourselves, and the truth is not in us. ⁹ If we confess our sins, he is faithful and just to forgive us our sins and to cleanse us from all unrighteousness. ¹⁰ If we say we have not sinned, we make him a liar, and his word is not in us.

Q: Do we really need Jesus to cleanse us from our sin?

Q: What does it mean to confess our sins?

Q: What does it mean to be cleansed all from sin? What would that feel like?

Removing Sin

Psalm 103:11-13

[11] For as high as the heavens are above the earth,

    so great is his steadfast love toward those who fear him;

[12] as far as the east is from the west,

    so far does he remove our transgressions (sins) from us.

[13] As a father shows compassion to his children,

    so the Lord shows compassion to those who fear him.

Q: How far does God remove our sin from us?

Jeremiah 31:33-34

[33] For this is the covenant that I will make with the house of Israel after those days, declares the Lord: I will put my law within them, and I will write it on their hearts. And I will be their God, and they shall be my people. [34] And no longer shall each one teach his neighbor and each his brother, saying, 'Know the Lord,' for they shall all know me, from the least of them to the greatest, declares the Lord. For I will forgive their iniquity, and I will remember their sin no more."

Q: How is it possible for God to forget our sin?

Q: If God cleanses our hearts and forgets our sin, how does that affect our identity?

By Grace, Through Faith

Ephesians 2:8-10

[8] For by grace you have been saved through faith. And this is not your own doing; it is the gift of God, [9] not a result of works, so that no one may boast. [10] For we are his workmanship, created in Christ Jesus for good works, which God prepared beforehand, that we should walk in them.

Romans 5:1-2

[1] Therefore, since we have been justified by faith, we have peace with God through our Lord Jesus Christ. [2] Through him we have also obtained access by faith into this grace in which we stand, and we rejoice in hope of the glory of God.

Q: What is grace?

Q: How can we access the grace of God?

Q: So what is faith?

> In Scripture, the Greek word translated as *faith* means to be persuaded or to be convinced. In simple terms, faith is being confident in our hearts that what God says is really true.

Faith of the Heart

Romans 10:8-10

[8] But what does it say? "The word is near you, in your mouth and in your heart" (that is, the word of faith that we proclaim); [9] because, if you confess with your mouth that Jesus is Lord and believe in your heart that God raised him from the dead, you will be saved. [10] For with the heart one believes and is justified, and with the mouth one confesses and is saved.

Q: What does it mean to believe with our hearts?

Q: What does this say about intellectual belief?

Q: How can we tell the difference between head-knowledge (intellectual belief) and heart-knowledge (faith)?

Q: How do we get genuine faith? How do we get true heart-knowledge?

Summary

"To be saved from our sin is a gift of God's love. There is nothing we can do to earn it. We simply believe—truly believe. We receive faith and confidence from God, and just enjoy the reality of being forgiven through Jesus and set free from sin.

When we believe something in our heart, our lives change. The way we think about God, ourselves, and the world around us, all changes. Our actions change. This change is called repentance. It is dying to our old life and living with Jesus. When we believe in Jesus and are prepared to turn from our old life, we can express our faith through baptism. Through baptism we publicly declare that we have joined our lives to Jesus and we will be united with Him in death and in life. Our new life has begun and it's a cause for celebration!

10 | Home Reading and Questions

☐ **Hebrews 4:1-3**

I: Imagine what it would be like to experience spiritual rest—the end of stress and striving, and instead having a sense of continual peace.

Q: Has God given me a promise of entering into rest?

Q: What does it mean to come short of the promise?

Q: How can I hear the word of God and have faith?

Q: Do I want to receive the gift of faith?

☐ **Hebrews 12:1-2**

Q: Why did Jesus endure the cross?

Q: What was the joy set before Him?

Q: Could Jesus find joy in me?

Q: What does it mean for Jesus to be the author of my faith?

Q: What does it mean for Jesus to be the perfecter of my faith?

☐ **Romans 1:16-17**
Q: How is the gospel the power of salvation?

Q: What would it mean for me to live by faith?

☐ **Acts 3:17-21**
Q: What does it me for me to "repent and return"?

Q: Can't I just believe and be forgiven without needing to repent?

Q: What would it be like to be refreshed in the presence of God?

☐ **Acts 4-5**
Write down your questions here:

☐ **Experiences with God**

Write down your some of your own prayers, discoveries, questions and experiences.

11 | Born Again

John 3:3-8

[3] Now there was a man of the Pharisees named Nicodemus, a ruler of the Jews. [2] This man came to Jesus by night and said to him, "Rabbi, we know that you are a teacher come from God, for no one can do these signs that you do unless God is with him." [3] Jesus answered him, "Truly, truly, I say to you, unless one is born again he cannot see the kingdom of God." [4] Nicodemus said to him, "How can a man be born when he is old? Can he enter a second time into his mother's womb and be born?" [5] Jesus answered, "Truly, truly, I say to you, unless one is born of water and the Spirit, he cannot enter the kingdom of God. [6] That which is born of the flesh is flesh, and that which is born of the Spirit is spirit. [7] Do not marvel that I said to you, 'You must be born again.' [8] The wind blows where it wishes, and you hear its sound, but you do not know where it comes from or where it goes. So it is with everyone who is born of the Spirit."

Q: What does it mean to be born of water?

Q: What does it mean to be born of the Spirit?

John 1:29-33 (John the Baptist speaking)

[29] The next day he saw Jesus coming toward him, and said, "Behold, the Lamb of God, who takes away the sin of the world! [30] This is he of whom I said, 'After me comes a man who ranks before me, because he was before me.' [31] I myself did not know him,

but for this purpose I came baptizing with water, that he might be revealed to Israel."
[32] And John bore witness: "I saw the Spirit descend from heaven like a dove, and it remained on him. [33] I myself did not know him, but he who sent me to baptize with water said to me, 'He on whom you see the Spirit descend and remain, this is he who baptizes with the Holy Spirit.'

Q: Baptize is a Greek word meaning *immerse.* What does it mean to be immersed in the Spirit of Jesus?

Q: What would be mean for our hearts to be soaked through with the Spirit of Jesus?

Q: How do we get immersed in the Spirit?

The Image of God

Romans 8:28-30
[28] And we know that for those who love God all things work together for good, for those who are called according to his purpose. [29] For those whom he foreknew he also predestined to be conformed to the image of his Son, in order that he might be the firstborn among many brothers. [30] And those whom he predestined he also called, and those whom he called he also justified, and those whom he justified he also glorified.

"" The Greek word *proorizo* translated as *predestined* has the sense of designing or defining a plan. Unlike the English word *predestined, proorizo* is not limited to a future destiny, but it also speaks of a present experience. Being conformed to the image of Jesus is something that we can experience now, in this life.

Q: What does it mean to conform something?

Q: What does it mean to be conformed to the image of Jesus?

Q: What is the image of Jesus like?

Q: How are we conformed to the image of Jesus?

2 Corinthians 3:17-18

[17] Now the Lord is the Spirit, and where the Spirit of the Lord is, there is freedom. [18] And we all, with unveiled face, beholding the glory of the Lord, are being transformed into the same image from one degree of glory to another. For this comes from the Lord who is the Spirit.

Q: Who is the Spirit of God?

Q: What does it mean to be transformed?

Q: What does it mean: from glory to glory?

Q: So how does it all happen? How are we transformed by the Spirit of Jesus?

Regeneration

Titus 3:4-7
⁴ But when the goodness and loving kindness of God our Savior appeared, ⁵ he saved us, not because of works done by us in righteousness, but according to his own mercy, by the washing of regeneration and renewal of the Holy Spirit, ⁶ whom he poured out on us richly through Jesus Christ our Savior, ⁷ so that being justified by his grace we might become heirs according to the hope of eternal life.

Q: What is regeneration?

Summary

If we are to follow Jesus, we need to be born again, in water and Spirit. We need to be prepared to let Jesus bring death to our old-self through the cross, and bring new life to us through His Spirit. We make a public statement of our choice to die with Christ to sin and to live in unity with Him when we are baptized in water. The baptism of water is a symbol of the end of the old life and the beginning of a new life in relationship with God.

When Jesus fills us with His Spirit, we receive the power to live in unity with Him—the power to love with His love, to work with His power, and to live in reality through His truth. With the Spirit we receive a new image for our lives, a new identity and design. This is the gift that Jesus offers us: a whole new life in relationship with Him. The gift has been given and it is our choice to receive it or not.

11 | Home Reading and Questions

☐ **Romans 8:31-37**

I: Imagine living a life saturated in the love of Jesus. Imagine that nothing could separate you from His love. Imagine going through the difficulties of life, even dangers and loss, but always having the love of Jesus with you. Imagine overwhelmingly overcoming every challenge in life, all through the love of Jesus.

Q: What would it feel like to know that God is for me?

Q: Does God really want to freely give me everything I need?

Q: What can separate me from the love of Jesus?

Q: How can I know more of God's love for me?

☐ **John 15:1-11**

I: Imagine a vine. Imagine the nutrients and life of the vine, flowing through to the branches. Imagine the fruit growing on the branches.

Q: What does it mean for me to be connected to Jesus?

Q: What does it mean for Jesus' words to abide in me?

Q: What would it be like to have the joy of Jesus in my heart?

☐ **John 15:12-17**

Q: How can I love other people like Jesus loves me?

Q: What does it mean for me to be a friend of God?

Q: Has Jesus chosen me?

Q: Have I chosen Jesus?

☐ **Acts 6-7**

Write down your questions here:

☐ **Experiences with God**

Write down your some of your own prayers, discoveries, questions and experiences.

12 | A New Beginning

Eternal Life

John 3:16
For God so loved the world, that he gave his only Son, that whoever believes in him should not perish but have eternal life.

Q: What does it mean to believe in Jesus?

" The original Greek wording for this passage says that whoever believes *into* Jesus should not perish but have eternal life *right now and into the* future (communicated through the Greek present tense). So eternal life starts as soon as we begin to believe into Jesus and continues for all eternity.

Q: What does it mean to believe *into* Jesus*?*

Q: So what is eternal life?

The Only Way

John 14:6
Jesus said to him, "I am the way, and the truth, and the life. No one comes to the Father except through me."

Q: Why is Jesus the only way to the Father?

Matthew 7:13-14
[13] "Enter by the narrow gate. For the gate is wide and the way is easy that leads to destruction, and those who enter by it are many. [14] For the gate is narrow and the way is hard that leads to life, and those who find it are few.

Q: We know that Jesus is the only way, but what does He say about the way here?

Q: Why is it hard to choose to follow Jesus?

Q: What is the cost of following Jesus?

Counting the Cost

Mark 12:28-33

[28] And one of the scribes came up and heard them disputing with one another, and seeing that he answered them well, asked him, "Which commandment is the most important of all?" [29] Jesus answered, "The most important is, 'Hear, O Israel: The Lord our God, the Lord is one. [30] And you shall love the Lord your God with all your heart and with all your soul and with all your mind and with all your strength.' [31] The second is this: 'You shall love your neighbor as yourself.' There is no other commandment greater than these." [32] And the scribe said to him, "You are right, Teacher. You have truly said that he is one, and there is no other besides him. [33] And to love him with all the heart and with all the understanding and with all the strength, and to love one's neighbor as oneself, is much more than all whole burnt offerings and sacrifices."

Q: What does this passage show us about following Jesus?

Q: Is there a cost to loving God and loving others?

Matthew 10:37-39

[37] "Whoever loves father or mother more than me is not worthy of me, and whoever loves son or daughter more than me is not worthy of me. [38] And whoever does not take his cross and follow me is not worthy of me. [39] Whoever finds his life will lose it, and whoever loses his life for my sake will find it."

Q: Why is it so important to love Jesus more than anyone or anything?

Q: What does it mean to lose our life if we find it and find it when we lose it?

John 15:17-20

[17] "These things I command you, so that you will love one another. [18] If the world hates you, know that it has hated me before it hated you. [19] If you were of the world, the world would love you as its own; but because you are not of the world, but I chose you out of the world, therefore the world hates you. [20] Remember the word that I said to you: 'A servant is not greater than his master.' If they persecuted me, they will also persecute you. If they kept my word, they will also keep yours."

Q: What is the promise that is made in this passage?

Q: What could be the cost for us?

Q: What is the reward of following Jesus? What's the benefit?

Q: So will it be worth the cost?

Day of Salvation

I Corinthians 5:14 – 6:10

[14] For the love of Christ controls us, because we have concluded this: that one has died for all, therefore all have died; [15] and he died for all, that those who live might no longer live for themselves but for him who for their sake died and was raised.

[16] From now on, therefore, we regard no one according to the flesh. Even though we once regarded Christ according to the flesh, we regard him thus no longer. [17] Therefore, if anyone is in Christ, he is a new creation. The old has passed away; behold, the new has come. [18] All this is from God, who through Christ reconciled us to himself and gave us the ministry of reconciliation; [19] that is, in Christ God was reconciling the world to himself, not counting their trespasses against them, and entrusting to us the message of reconciliation. [20] Therefore, we are ambassadors for Christ, God making his appeal through us. We implore you on behalf of Christ, be reconciled to God. [21] For our sake he made him to be sin who knew no sin, so that in him we might become the righteousness of God.

[6:1] Working together with him, then, we appeal to you not to receive the grace of God in vain. [2] For he says, "In a favorable time I listened to you, and in a day of salvation I have helped you."

Behold, now is the favorable time; behold, now is the day of salvation. [3] We put no obstacle in anyone's way, so that no fault may be found with our ministry, [4] but as servants of God we commend ourselves in every way: by great endurance, in afflictions, hardships, calamities, [5] beatings, imprisonments, riots, labors, sleepless nights, hunger; [6] by purity, knowledge, patience, kindness, the Holy Spirit, genuine love; [7] by truthful speech, and the power of God; with the weapons of righteousness for the right hand and for the left; [8] through honor and dishonor, through slander and praise. We are treated as impostors, and yet are true; [9] as unknown, and yet well known; as dying, and behold, we live; as punished, and yet not killed; [10] as sorrowful, yet always rejoicing; as poor, yet making many rich; as having nothing, yet possessing everything.

Q: Do we want to be made into a new creation?

Q: When is the day of salvation?

"
Jesus is offering each one of you the gift of His love and presence and eternal life. Please don't receive the grace of God in vain. Today is the day of your salvation. He has designed you. He has called you by name. He has chosen you. What is your response? If you haven't already, will you give your life to Jesus? Will you follow Him?

12 | Home Reading and Questions

☐ **Hebrews 10:12-17**
Q: How great was Jesus' sacrifice to conquer sin?

Q: Can any sin remain after being washed by the blood of Jesus?

Q: If the Law of God is love, what would it be like to have God's law written on my heart and mind?

☐ **2 Timothy 3:10-17**
Q: What does God promise in this passage?

Q: Why must persecutions come to people who just want to live a godly life in Christ?

Q: What does it mean for me to continue on in the things I have become convinced of?

☐ **Ephesians 1:15-22**

Q: What would it be like to receive a spirit of wisdom and revelation in the knowledge of Jesus?

Q: What is the hope of my calling?

Q: What are the riches of glory of my inheritance in Jesus?

Q: What would it be like for me to experience the surpassing power of Jesus?

Q: Is there anything that can stand against God's power in Jesus?

☐ **Prayer** *Write your own prayer to Jesus here:*

☐ **Acts 6-7**

Write down your questions here:

☐ Experiences with God

Write down your some of your own prayers, discoveries, questions and experiences.

Introduction to the Bible

The Bible is made up of 66 books written by about 40 different people over a period of 1600 years. What makes the Bible different to other books is that God Himself is the ultimate Author. He inspired the authors of each book to accurately record His word. So the Bible itself says that all Scripture (writings in the Bible) is "God breathed" (2 Timothy 3:16). God Himself is telling His story through the Bible.

What's it all about?

The Bible is a love story between a Creator and the people He created, set over thousands of years. In the Bible, God reveals who He is. He shares His heart and tells of His unfailing love, His promises and gifts, and His awesome greatness. He also shows us who He created us to be, and how He has made it possible for us to know and love Him as He originally intended.

The main character of the Bible is Jesus Christ. It is His story because He is the central focus of the love between God and man. He is the Son of God who gave His life to wash away all our sin and failings and bring us back into relationship with our Creator. He is the divine Bridegroom, looking to share His love with us as His bride.

Navigating the Bible

The Bible is divided into two parts, which are known as the Old and New Testament. The Old Testament is made up of 39 books and is all about the promises that God makes with His chosen people, Israel. It begins with creation and records the history of God's relationship with Israel up until 400 years before the birth of Jesus. Even though Jesus appeared centuries after the Old Testament was written, prophecies (messages foretelling the future) about him can be found all through the Old Testament.

The promises that God made to Israel were ultimately fulfilled in Jesus. The New Testament tells us about the life of Jesus, His death and resurrection, and reveals how He made it possible for everyone to live as God's people. The New Testament is made up of 27 books which begin just before the birth of Jesus and end with a prophetic look into the future at the ultimate universal reign of Jesus Christ as Lord of All.

Books of the Bible

Genesis → Deuteronomy - *Books of Moses*

These books record life from Creation to Israel's entry into the Promised Land

Joshua → Esther - *Books of History*

These books cover Israel's history from its first possession of the Promised Land, to its exile into Assyria and Babylon and to its return back to the land.

Job → Song of Songs - *Books of Poetry*

These books deal with different subjects ranging from the sovereignty and faithfulness of God, to the pain of suffering and loss, to the celebration of love.

Isaiah -> Malachi - *Books of Prophecy*

These books speak prophetically, which means that they are the voice of God to His people, often speaking of things to come. Many times in these books, Jesus' birth, death and resurrection are foretold.

Matthew → John - *The Gospels*

These books record the life of Jesus, His death and resurrection.

Acts -> *Early Church History*

This book records the early days of the Church.

Romans → Jude - *Letters*

These letters were written to teach and encourage believers in the early churches.

Revelation - *Prophecy*

This book takes a look at events surrounding the eternal reign of Jesus.

A Brief History

God created the universe and the world we live in. He created Adam and Eve in His image. However Adam and Eve rebelled against God and denied His image within them. Instead they chose to follow self rather than God. We all did this at sometime in our lives: we all acted selfishly and rejected God's design for our lives.

However, God's plan has always been to restore people back into His image and all creation to its original glory. So He set in motion His plan of redemption.

Around 2000 B.C. God called a man named Abraham to leave his home in Syria and move to Canaan. God promised Abraham that He would bless the world through one of Abraham's descendants. Abraham fathered Isaac who fathered Jacob who was renamed Israel. Israel's son Joseph was taken as a captive to Egypt, and eventually the whole family of Israel resettled in Egypt. Over a period of about 500 years, the families of Israel's sons grew and became a numerous nation, which later became known simply as *Israel*. During their time in Egypt, the whole nation became enslaved by the Egyptian authorities.

The slavery in Egypt was harsh and God's people cried out for deliverance. About 1400 B.C. God sent Moses to lead Israel's descendants out of Egypt and into Canaan. During their journey, God gave Moses His Law, which is found in the first five books of the Bible. The Law was based on loving God and loving others, and included many promises from God. If the people would love God and each other and not follow the ways of the world then they would live in blessing and prosper. However, if they abandoned a life of love and took on other gods then they would forfeit the land and the nationhood that God had promised to them.

Moses died before entering into Canaan and so Joshua led Israel into their Promised Land. There was a time of conquest during which God made a way for His people, often miraculously clearing the nations before them. Once settled in the land, the people of Israel were governed by a number of judges. Eventually the people decided that they wanted a king so God gave them a man called Saul to rule as king. About 1000 B.C David became Israel's king in the place of Saul. During the reigns of David and his son Solomon, Israel grew into a prosperous and powerful kingdom. God reaffirmed the promise He gave to Abraham by promising David and Solomon that a descendant of theirs would one day rise to reign as a king for all eternity.

The nation of Israel was made up of 12 tribes. After Solomon's reign ended, the nation of Israel had an internal split. The ten northern tribes remained united and called themselves *Israel*. After around 200 years, the ten tribes of Israel forfeited the land on account of their relentless idolatry. The Assyrian army came and conquered Israel about 721 B.C. and led the people as slaves back to Assyria.

The two southern tribes were known as *Judah,* which is where we get the term *Jew.* God saved Judah from the Assyrian conquest that had defeated the northern tribes. However, it was not long before Judah also turned from God and abandoned the ways of love. Because of their idolatry, Judah was conquered by the Babylonian army and taken as captives to Babylon around 600 B.C.

The Persian Empire rose to power and overcame Babylon. Around 70 years after Judah's capture, the Persian king allowed some of God's people to return to their land. Jerusalem, the capital, was rebuilt about 444 B.C. during the time of Nehemiah and Ezra. The Jewish people once again established a national identity as Israel.

After this there was a time of relative quiet for Israel, during which the Greek Empire rose (overcoming Persia in the process) and then fell to the Roman Empire. During the Roman rule, Jesus Christ was born in Bethlehem.

Jesus was the chosen descendant that God spoke of in His promises to Abraham, Isaac, Israel, David and Solomon. Jesus was the Messiah—the King of glory, who would reign as King all eternity. Jesus was the Righteous One who lived His entire life in obedience to the ways of God's love. Jesus was also the Lamb of God who would give His life to take away sin from His people and restore them back into the image of God.

Jesus died on the cross, defeating sin and selfishness. He was then raised from the dead, defeating death itself. Through the death and resurrection of Jesus, God made a new covenant with all people, not just Israel. Absolutely anyone who believes into Jesus will be saved from sin and given the gift of eternal life in Christ.

Not long after His resurrection, Jesus released the power and presence of His Spirit upon His disciples. Through the power of Jesus' Spirit and their eye-witness testimony of His death and resurrection, Jesus' followers travelled all over the known world sharing the good news of salvation, love and eternal life through Jesus Christ. The Bible closes with a revelation of Jesus' return to judge the world and restore all creation back into its awesome glory.

discoverjesus.today

www.ingramcontent.com/pod-product-compliance
Lightning Source LLC
Chambersburg PA
CBHW081255040426
42452CB00014B/2505